Notes from a Titus Woman

The A-Z of Caring
For Your Family and Home

Mo Mydlo

We'd love to hear from you about your experience with this book. Please follow me on my blog at **www.momydlo.wordpress.com**. Title: Unforsaken

 Unforsaken by Mo Mydlo

 Twitter@momydlo

Mydlo, Mo, 1973 –
    Notes from a Titus Woman: The A – Z of caring for your home and family /
    Mo Mydlo

ISBN-13: 978-1478101499
ISBN-10: 1478101490

This book is dedicated to my two favorite disciples:
Angel Clark and Sara Mydlo.
You two girls have given me a newfound passion
to live as though Someone is always watching.
I love you both so much and I pray God's blessings
on you and your families for years to come.

Introduction

Times continue to change drastically for new wives and mothers. Many women find themselves seeking for wisdom anywhere they can find it where raising their family is concerned. There are so many different opinions at our fingertips to choose from. It is often overwhelming for us.

In years past, the extended family lived with or within walking distance of other relatives, giving them the encouragement, education and confidence they require in raising Godly children. Unfortunately, this is rare today.

The Bible has much to say to women about parenting and homemaking. It truly is the guidebook to life for every issue. But, with every bit of education, a teacher is required. In the book of Titus, God lays out specifically who needs to be teaching these young women how to live righteously as wives and mothers. It is the older women. I like to refer to them as "Titus women", especially because I am officially one of them now, and the word "older" just never seems to stroke the ego.

Titus 2:3-5 says, *"Likewise, teach the older women to be reverent in the way they live, not to be slanderers or addicted to much wine, but to teach what is good. Then they can train the younger women to love their husbands and children, to be self-controlled and pure, to be busy at home, to be kind, and to be subject to their husbands, so that no one will malign the Word of God."*

I chose to write this book in a simple A to Z fashion mainly because, as wives and mothers, we are so busy that we need literature that can be digested in small cubits of time, but prove to make a huge impact. Each letter of the alphabet represents a life lesson that I have learned - mostly the hard way. I pray that you take God's Word as absolute truth and apply it to your life, so that you can learn it the easy way.

You see, most of the lessons and tests God gives us throughout life do allow retakes, but those retakes usually come after struggles because we didn't study, or we didn't listen to the teacher. My prayer is that you enjoy reading this book, studying the material, and passing the test the first time because summer school is a bummer!

God bless you,

Mo

A

Always

ALWAYS PUT GOD FIRST BY GETTING UP BEFORE YOUR FAMILY AND SPENDING TIME WITH GOD AND IN HIS WORD.

Proverbs 31:15
She gets up while it is still dark.

You may think that there will be plenty of time during the day to get alone with God, but there always seems to be distractions and responsibilities once other members of the family are all awake. There is such a special chemistry between God and man early in the a.m. God will speak to you in a still small voice. He is a gentleman, and he won't barge the door down to your heart or scream over all of your busyness. It is important that you give Him the first fruits of your day.

God can show us how to manage our day with grace, dignity and peace if we will obey His commands to put Him first in everything. That includes our schedules. I want to encourage you to allow God to be the director of your daily To-Do lists.

The woman in Proverbs 31 knew that in order to accomplish all that she needed to, she would need to allow time in her schedule for the King of Kings to lead. We need to follow her lead, and watch God move in our lives. Set your alarm clock, and ignore the desire to roll over and hit the snooze button. The comfort of our Heavenly Father beats our favorite pillow and blanket any day. You can do it!

B

Balance

IN ORDER TO SUCCEED AS A GODLY WIFE AND MOTHER, YOU MUST LEARN HOW TO BALANCE WORK AND PLAY

Ecclesiastes 3:13
That everyone may eat and drink, and find satisfaction in all of his toil - this is the gift of God.

Your job as a wife and mother can sometimes be an exhausting one. You need to schedule interactive play each day with your children. Reading, make-believe, outdoor and rough and tumble play should all be part of your child's daily routine.

It is your job as a mother to make sure all of these necessary activities happen. The television should not be used to replace playtime, but can be useful for teaching when it is time to rest. You will just need to be serious about monitoring what they watch and for how long.

Children learn how to be adults by pretending to be adults through make-believe as children. Encourage their imagination as they play with other children, alone, and with you. Play with your kids. Have joyful, happy, fun together, and then use clean-up time as a lesson in learning responsibility. Everything in life is more manageable when balance is maintained. When children are taught how to work and play, both aspects can become easily ingrained into their spirit as they grow. Play and have fun, then you can clean up the playroom together!

C

Cooking

COOKING IS AN ART THAT ANYONE CAN MASTER!

John 6:51
"I am the living bread that comes down from Heaven.
If anyone eats of this bread, they will live forever.
This bread is my flesh, which I will give for the life of
the world."

Does the subject of cooking burden you? I think cooking lessons should be a pre-requisite for every new wife and mother. Today, Home Economics courses have been cut from school budgets and, because of the convenience of fast food and eating out, our health, and the joy of the family dinner, have both suffered. We can turn this around and bring back the much-needed staple of cooking to the family.

I would suggest you make a list of everything you know how to cook and everything that you desire to learn how to cook, and have fun learning. Mothers, grandmothers, aunts and friends love sharing their favorite recipes with the people they love. If you do not know anyone nearby who can cook, get your mom on the phone and ask her to teach you by phone, or sign up for a cooking course at your local community college. If you are a mother who already loves to cook, get your children involved. As you are baking a pie or stirring gravy, show your children what you are doing. Children learn by example. Try handing them the spoon and asking them to stir the batter.

This not only fills your child's need for quality time with you, it is also a form of apprenticeship into adulthood that they will pass on to your grandchildren someday. Let's get out the utensils we got for Christmas and start cooking!

D

Discipline

DISCIPLINE IS LOVE!

Proverbs 10:18
Discipline your son, for in that there is hope.

Discipline needs to begin when your children are very young. Discipline should not be harsh, abusive or exasperate your children. It should involve consistent rules set in place and consequences carried out for breaking these rules. Discipline gives your children their first sense of safety, boundaries and protection. Children learn self-control and emotional management by growing up in a family that enforces healthy discipline.

For younger children, the Time-Out Spot seemed to work well in our family. The method is very simple, but you must be consistent for it to be effective. The child is given one warning, and then if they choose to ignore that warning, they are placed into a time-out while they think about their actions. A good rule to use in figuring out the duration of time-out is one-minute for each year of their age. I do not advocate standing near your child and lecturing them or talking to them while they are in time-out as that only enforces negative attention with them. Simply say to them, *"There is no talking in time-out"* and set the timer for the allotted punishment time.

When their time-out is finished, go to them and ask, *"Why did we have a time-out?"* Allow them to say what they did, then say, *"Are we going to try harder next time?"* When the answer is *"Yes"*, simply say *"Thank you"*. I always allow my children a chance to say *"I am sorry"* and I also always say, *"I forgive you"*. This is a healthy way for your children to understand grace and forgiveness, and allows them to forgive themselves and not harbor unnecessary guilt.

As your children grow, the Time-Out will obviously be less effective and can be replaced with some sort of grounding from their favorite media devices, phones or whatever their favorite "currency" is. The wonderful thing that you will notice is that if you are consistent with your discipline while they are small, you will rarely have to discipline when they are in their teen years. They will have understood that boundaries and rules are a good thing, and they will be a joy to be around. Yes, teenagers can be a joy! To discipline, is to love!

E

Eating

EAT DINNER TOGETHER AS A FAMILY!

Acts 2:46-47
Every day they continued to meet together in the temple courts. They broke bread in their homes and ate together with glad and sincere hearts, praising God and enjoying the favor of all the people.

The family dinner table should be a safe place to fall after a long day in a tough world. Your husband and children, as well as you, should be free to talk, share joys and feel sorrows, to laugh and sometimes even cry together.

Assigned seats at the dinner table may sound too regimented to you, but to children, their seat at the dinner table represents their spot in the family. They have a say in matters, a voice that is not ignored, and a position in this business called "the family".

The preparation of the food, setting and clearing of the table and dishes allow responsibility to be taught, and important disciplines to be established.

A prayer of thankfulness at the beginning of each meal teaches us to remain grateful for basic needs such as food, clothing and shelter. After the prayer, my family enjoys a game of "High-Low" at each meal. One person goes, then after they tell their High and their Low (their favorite and worst parts of their day), they pass it to whoever they choose, until we all have gone. The kids know they have to have a High, even if it is just to be thankful to have daily breath of life.   But, a day without a Low is welcomed and celebrated anytime.   When my kids were younger, they would even pass it to their imaginary friends to do "High-Low" as they didn't want anyone to feel left out.

Even if your schedules become bogged down with sports and activities, guard your family dinner table time with diligence: for it undoubtedly is true: *A family that eats together, stays together.*

F

Feelings

YOUR FEELINGS LIE TO YOU SOMETIMES!

Proverbs 3:5-6
*Trust in the Lord with all of your heart
and lean not on your own understanding.
In all your ways acknowledge Him,
and He will make your path straight.*

As women, our feelings change like the wind. You cannot rely on your feelings to determine your actions. You must rely on the truths contained in God's Word. The Bible says, *"Trust in the Lord with all of your heart and lean not on your own understanding."* The Lord is specific about us not trusting in our own way of thinking as sometimes our understanding can be wrong. Mistakes of the past, hurts and regrets, and living in a fallen world can all distort the way God would want us to react to situations.

As women, we are emotional creatures, and we cannot allow our emotions to control how we handle life. You will not always "feel" in love with your husband, but you need to love him. You will not always "feel" like putting others' needs before yours but as a mother, you will have to do that daily. You will not always "feel" like caring for your home, but usually when we fight through our feelings and do the right thing, God blesses us with an amazing peace and joy that we could never find on our own.

We must allow the lessons God teaches in His Word to renew our mind to line up with these truths instead of trusting our feelings. Find out what God's Word says about being a wife and mother and it will help you to live a life based on truths, not on feelings!

G

God

GOD WILL NOT SHARE HIS THRONE!

Exodus 20:4-5
*You shall not make for yourself any idol
in the form of anything in Heaven above
or on earth beneath, or on the waters below.
You shall not bow down to them or worship them.*

As humans, it is our nature to worship. God built us that way to bring glory to his name. People in third-world countries who have never heard of Jesus find inanimate objects to worship. As believers, we must be very careful not to bow down to other objects in this world. These objects could be money, fame, sports, shopping, our spouses, or our children. We have a way of creating for ourselves a bunch of "little gods". These are what the Bible refers to as "idols". Idols can come in all shapes and sizes. Idols represent anything we give more attention to other than God himself.

God is a jealous God and He will not share your heart with a bunch of "little gods". You must realize where your priorities may be out of balance, how much glory you give to things other than God, and where you are bowing down and putting people and things only where God belongs, and cast down these idols.

Many parents struggle with making their children their idols. This is damaging because they will begin to believe that they are the center of the universe. When the real world shows them that they are not, it can become a very discouraging and harsh place to live. I would encourage you to teach your children at a very young age a serious respect for the living God. My children's first memory verse was *"The fear of the Lord is the beginning of knowledge."* Proverbs 1:7 When we keep God's throne for only Him, He blesses that humility more than you could ever imagine.

H

Home

HOME IS WHERE THE PEACE IS!

Philippians 2:14
Do everything without complaining or arguing.

Children and adults will naturally be drawn towards places of peace. I would encourage you to make every effort to keep your home visually, emotionally and relationally peaceful. I try to tidy my home daily so that when guests come through, or pop in, they do not feel uncomfortable sitting among clutter or chaos.

I think it is important not to argue in front of guests or reprimand your children in front of their friends or others. If your children require discipline while others are around, you can ask your guests to excuse you while you quietly take your child into another room and address their behavior. My husband and I made a pact early in our relationship to never embarrass each other in public. We have fallen short before and have had to repent, but it is our ongoing desire to build each other and our children up and not tear them down.

If you make your home a desired place to be, your children will bring their friends home with them where you can monitor what they are exposed to. This also gives you influence on your children's friends for Jesus. It can become a mission field in your very own home.

It is important to me that when my husband and the kids return home, the house is tidy, the snacks are available, and I am there to greet them to ask them about their day. Whether you are a stay at home mom, or a working mom, you can ask God for wisdom to accomplish this. Then your home will be where the peace is and where your family wants to be.

I

Insecurity

INSECURITY WILL KEEP YOU FROM YOUR PURPOSE!

John 3:16
For God so loved the world that He gave his one and only son, that whoever shall believe in Him shall not perish, but have eternal life.

Insecurity will keep you from your purpose. Do not make the mistake of comparing yourself to other women. Each woman has a purpose that God created just for her. God did not create any of us with a cookie cutter mold. He loves us too much to do that.

There will be many of you who decide to be working mothers, and others will stay home with their children. There will be many of you who decide to home educate your children, and others will decide private or public school is your best option. Some of you will be called to work actively in the ministry while others will be called to be prayer warriors at home. Some of you will be great housekeepers, and some of you will iron holes in your husband's shirts when you should be taking them to the cleaners to do.

Your worth and value as a mother does not come from

what the world says about you or by what you do. Your worth and value comes from Jesus and what He says about you, and that is this: *'I love you so much, that I am willing to die for you.'* The best part of that is Jesus backed what he said with actions. He did die for you, and He wants nothing more from you as a woman than for you to love Him in return. If you are a woman who has Jesus, you are woman who has everything.

J

Jesus

JESUS, NAME ABOVE ALL NAMES!

Deuteronomy 11:18-19
Fix these words of mine in your hearts and minds;
tie them as symbols on your hands
and bind them on your foreheads.
Teach them to your children,
talking about them when you sit at home
and when you walk along the road,
when you lie down, and when you get up.

Does the world know that your family loves the Lord? Do they look at you and see Jesus? Hear Jesus? Even, smell Jesus? Do you know that there will be a time in your walk with the Lord that the Bible says you will even have the *"aroma of Christ"*? Oh, how I want to smell like the Lord.

Jesus is my family's thing! It is our thing. We love Him. Some people love horses, or waterskiing, or mountain biking, or baseball. Those things are all great, but Jesus is our thing. My goal is to be a tool for the Lord to use anywhere I go, every day I breath, and in every creative way He chooses to use me.

Our home is a place where we choose to invite people to gather and feel welcome as the Lord is exalted through teaching, prayer or just plain fun. The Word of God is present in each room in this house. You see evidence everywhere, whether it is the invite to Easter service at our church posted on the refrigerator, or the bookshelf in my living room filled with Bible studies and devotionals, or my daughter's favorite scripture verse posted on her wall on an art canvas above her bed as a headboard. Our car even has a window cling advertising our local church. We are a walking billboard for the Lord, but with that come much responsibility.

If we choose to wear the garment of a Christian, we have to act like Jesus would to a lost world. We have to be available to help someone in need, give more than what is expected, treat people with loving kindness, and display love wherever we go. Too many people have blown their witness to the world as Christians by allowing their Christianity to be on display and then turning around and treating people badly. We need to get the world excited about Jesus by acting like Jesus! Won't you allow Jesus to be your family's thing?

K

Keep

KEEP YOUR COMMITMENTS!

Matthew 5:37
*Simply let your "yes" be "yes" and your '"no", "no",
anything beyond this comes from the evil one.*

Be very careful what you promise to do with and for your children. They will trust that as their parent, your word will be your bond and that you will do what you say you will do. Consistency and dependability build confidence in your children. The opposite holds true as well. Nothing will breed insecurity quicker than unpredictability.

Try not to overpromise things to your children if you are not sure if you can follow through. This could represent anything from saying you will be at your son's basketball game (when you are not quite sure if work will let you leave early), and then not showing up, to disciplining your child for an action one time, then ignoring the same action the next time. A lack of consistency is very confusing to a child.

We must be women of our word. Try not to be an over-promiser. Follow through with your commitments, and then watch your child's trust in you flourish and their confidence shine!

L

Love

LOVE COVERS A MULTITUDE OF SINS!

1Peter 4:8
Above all, love each other deeply,
because love covers a multitude of sins.

Do not get hung up on perfectionism. You will do wonderfully at some aspects of your job as wife and mother, and you may struggle in other areas. We all have certain gifts and talents that God has given us to use for his glory, but not one of us has all of them.

The Bible calls us to pursue holiness and we should be doing so, but we will never fully reach the pinnacle of perfection until we are home with Jesus. Please give yourself a huge break by realizing this right now: You are going to mess up sometimes. When you do mess up as a wife or mother, do not hesitate to ask your husband or child for their forgiveness. By doing so, you are teaching them about grace. You can overcome so many imperfections by just being real and loving your family deeply.

I would encourage you to make it your goal that every time your husband and children lie their heads down on their pillows at night, they go to bed knowing they are loved. You can show your family they are loved by telling them often that you love them, by doing nice things for them, by hugging them and by spending quality time with them.

Keep it real! Don't be afraid for your family to see you are imperfect! Love without ceasing!

M

Money

MANAGE YOUR MONEY WELL!

Proverbs 14:1
*A good man leaves an inheritance for his
children's children, but a sinner's wealth is stored up
for the righteous.*

My husband and I always joke and say, *"We never fight about money, because we have no money to fight about."* Our family has never been what the world refers to as wealthy. We rarely have had money in savings, and for many years we lived paycheck to paycheck.

The best advice we ever heard financially did not come until we had been married about 10 years and we learned about tithing. Tithing is the biblical principal of the first 10% of your money going right back to the Lord. At the time that we were introduced to this, the thought of 10% more, coming out of our budget while still being responsible for our bills seemed like an impossible feat. When we finally decided to take the plunge and trust God with our finances, we witnessed some supernatural things happen. Exact amounts of money that we would need would show up, numbers would miraculously work in our favor, and there would be no explanation for these financial provisions except that it was the hand of God!

Tithing is such a serious thing to God that it is one of the only times in His Word in which he says, *'Test me with this.'* We did, and God showed himself worthy as usual. Our family has been tithing now for 10 years and we will do so as a family until The Lord calls us home. If you are struggling with finances, this simple formula can prove to put you in excellent financial standing when done diligently.

When you receive any income, take 10% and give it immediately back to God, then 10% goes directly into savings or to pay down debt, and use the remaining 80% to live on.

There are excellent Bible studies that you can do as a family that touch on biblical principles for finances. Read what God says about tithing in Malachi 3:7-12. Do not fret about money. Trust God, and watch Him move!

N

Never

NEVER QUIT!

Hebrews 12:1
*Therefore, since we are surrounded by
such a great cloud of witnesses,
let us throw off everything that hinders,
and the sin that so easily entangles,
and let us run with perseverance
the race marked out for us.*

Raising positive kids in a negative world is difficult, but possible. The one thing that we can never do is quit! There will be days when your children shine like stars in a dark world, and then there will be days that they will do everything that they can to be invisible among their peers.

Life in this world is not easy, and as Christians, the Bible says we sometimes will feel like we are aliens here. That is okay because our eternal home is something much greater and more spectacular than here. While we are here, though, we are to make a difference for Jesus.

It is possible to raise children today who can keep their eyes on the prize of pleasing the Lord. Do not believe the lie that all kids will try drugs and have premarital sex. Your children can remain pure and present themselves to their future spouses untarnished by the world, but they cannot do it without much prayer and study of God's word. As your child's parent, the best way you can teach them is by being a living example around them. Children raised by parents who do not abuse alcohol and drugs will not struggle as hard fighting these temptations themselves. Children raised by parents who dress modestly will not struggle as hard with appropriate dress. Children who are talked to about purity, encouraged in their purity, and taught in God's Word why they are to remain pure have a better chance of fighting lust than children whose parents avoid the conversation all together.

O

Open

OPEN YOUR BLINDS!

Psalm 27:1
The Lord is my light, and my salvation.

Have you ever noticed that the things that bother us in the night can somehow fade when the first light of morning hits? The scripture *"Sorrow may last for the night, but joy comes in the morning"* makes perfect sense.

Sunshine was created for a purpose. Nothing grows without the sun, including us. The sun sheds light in the darkness, warms our bones, and somehow sooths our souls. If you recognize yourself desiring to keep your blinds closed, blocking out the natural light, and hiding, maybe something is broken that needs fixing. Are you hiding a messy house that desperately needs a cleaning? Are you hiding from the neighbors who God so desperately wants us to reach out to? Are you hiding some hurts inside that desperately need mending? I want to encourage you to open the blinds and let the healing begin. You will recognize your houseplants bending towards the light. Living things desire light to thrive, and we are a living being. Each morning, the first thing I do is open my blinds. It is my way of saying, *"Ok, Lord, something good is going to happen to me today. I just know it."* Natural light in your home not only saves energy, it can save you from feeling depressed as well.

If you are a mom, take your children outside a little bit every day whether it is summer or winter. Children are energy producers. They need sunlight and fresh air to thrive and grow. Nothing makes me sadder than to see children not able to go outside to run, ride bikes, climb trees, fly kites, and play. Your children stay healthier, behave better, and sleep sounder when they have had a healthy amount of outdoor time each day. If it is a rainy day, let them go outside for a while in their new rain coat and boots and jump in some puddles. If it is sunny and hot, let them play in the garden hose! Fresh air and sunlight are crucial for all of us. OPEN THE BLINDS!

P

Proverbs

PROVERBS TEACH WISDOM!

Proverbs 1:7
*The fear of the Lord is the beginning of knowledge,
but fools despise wisdom and discipline.*

If you are a new student of the Word of God, what better place to start than the book of Proverbs? There are 31 Proverbs and 31 days in most months. You can read one Proverb a day and continue for the rest of your life, and still be gaining more and more knowledge. God's Word is alive and active, and whenever I read it, it seems to relate more and more to what I am dealing with.

Wisdom is something we need to be constantly seeking. There is always something to learn about parenting, mothering and about living as a Godly woman. As Christ followers, we need to be seeking wisdom at every turn. Wisdom can come from other people teaching you. It can come from books that you read, courses that you take, and lessons that you learn on your own. God's Word says in James 1:5, *"If any of you lacks wisdom, he should ask God, who gives generously to all, without finding fault, and it will be given to him."* Yes, God wants us to ask Him for wisdom through prayer and study of His Word.

I make it a habit to always be reading some sort of Christian literature (non-fiction). I make sure I am studying somewhere in the Bible, and if I am struggling to find where to dive in, I ask God, and He points me to Proverbs until I can figure out my next steps in my walk with Christ.

Grab a good cup of coffee, sit down in your favorite chair with your favorite blanket, and open to Proverbs. In all of your getting, get understanding! You will be glad you did.

Q

Question

QUESTION EVERYTHING!

Hebrews 4:12
For the Word of God is living and active.
Sharper than any double edged sword,
it penetrates to even dividing soul and spirit,
joints and marrow, it judges the
thoughts and attitudes of the heart.

Question everything with, *"Does this line up with the Word of God?"* You will be exposed to so many different teachings, practices and techniques as a wife and mother. Many people will give you advice, but it is crucial that you take every situation to God in prayer. Your feelings will even confuse you. If you are questioning whether feelings that you are having are from God or not, take them to prayer and study, and God will reveal truths to you.

Perhaps you are feeling like dressing pretty for a certain man at work since your husband has been kind of ignoring you lately, and this man has paid you some positive attention. What does the Word say? The Word says, *"Flee from sexual immorality!"* Do yourself a favor and stay as far away from this man as you can, and follow God's Word to stay faithful to your husband. Perhaps you are feeling like spending hours on the internet or on a social network instead of cleaning your house or spending time with your family. What does the Word say the younger women are to be doing? It says "to be self-controlled and pure, to be busy at home, to be kind, and to be subject to their husbands." Sometimes too much time on the internet or on our phones, can keep us from our calling as wives and mothers.

Perhaps you are feeling like practicing some New Age habits or worship such as visiting a psychic or reading a horoscope. What does the Word of God say about these practices? *"Anyone who does these things is detestable to the Lord. And, because of these detestable practices, The Lord your God will drive out nations before you."*

We must make sure that everything from the teaching we receive to the media we digest line up with the Word of God. If it does not, it usually will not have God's blessing attached to it. We are to guard our hearts with all diligence.

Question Everything!

R

Read

READ TOGETHER!

Revelation 1:3
*Blessed is the one who reads the words of this prophesy,
and blessed are those who hear it and take to heart
what is written in it, because the time is near.*

Reading together as a family can be such a treasured moment for all of you. Whether you read as a group or one on one in special settings, reading can be a blessed time for any family. Sometimes your kids will not get very excited about reading, so it is up to you as the parent to find fun ways to get them on board with this life skill.

Each summer, it is our goal to not "get a little dumber". That is our family's fun way of expressing our intent to "keep our minds strong". So we try to incorporate family reading time into our schedule. We love to have family dinner together then take an evening walk, and maybe all sit in the living room after and just find something fun to read. Even if it is the latest glamour magazine or a sports blog, it is simply a chance to exercise that brain muscle.

Something that my kids and I have all enjoyed are what we call "book picnics". We created these when we used to home school, and mommy was getting a little claustrophobic looking at the same four walls each day. We would grab a big blanket, find a cozy spot in the shade and head outside with a pile of books to read together under a tree. If it was a rainy day and a book picnic was required, the living room rug would suffice. But, we still would have to lay out that blanket for dramatic effect.

A love for reading isn't always established overnight. Sometimes and with some kids it will take years and a couple of really great teachers in school to get your kids excited about reading. But as their mommy, you are their first teacher and you need to influence them as early as possible with this pastime.

A love for reading isn't always established overnight. Sometimes and with some kids it will take years and a couple of really great teachers in school to get your kids excited about reading. But as their mommy, you are their first teacher and you need to influence them as early as possible with this pastime.

My desire for my kids to be avid readers is not so they can become puffed up scholars, it is to give them the tools they need in order to desire to devour the Word of God. They will need to possess the skills of reading, to be able to tackle the guidebook of life. You will never regret sewing this seed in their life.

S

Scheduling

SCHEDULE A PLAN!

Isaiah 32:8
But the noble man makes noble plans,
and by noble deeds he stands.

There is no doubt that the most successful individuals in life are those who create some sort of written plans or goals for their lives. Though sometimes amazing revelations are laid in our laps and seem to just take off, I believe usually God is working the hardest in the lives of those workmen who attempt to develop some sort of blueprint for their future.

Though God is truly in control, we need to be responsible for our half of our destiny. It is important that we develop systems, learn how to manage our time and resources well, and set schedules that can allow us to hear from God and put His plan into action in our lives.

Yes, we would all love to lie in bed and just wait for God to give us the revelation we want for the day, then head out to the raft in the pool and wait for the next great piece of literature that He wants to pen through us, but usually God is working through people who are moving!

Make sure your family has some sort of yearly goals

that you would like to accomplish. We like to create these together as a family right around New Years each year. Whether it is to read through the entire Old Testament as a family, or take a trip to the Bahamas on Spring Break, we love to write these goals down then look at them at the end of the year, and see which ones came to fruition.

One important tool in our house is the family calendar on the fridge. All sports schedules, school events, field trips, etc. must make their way to the family calendar in order for us to live organized lives. It is amazing how your event written on the calendar can give you a feeling of belonging to a family unit. We must be okay if the plan has to change as God remains in control of our everything, but I believe He is glorified when His people are not stagnant because of disorganization.

T

Talk

TALK ABOUT YOUR DAY!

Hebrews 3:13
*But encourage one another daily,
as long as it is called Today,
so that none of you may be hardened
by sin's deceitfulness.*

As a family, it is your job to encourage each other, defend each other and build each other up as you carry the gospel to a hurting world. Living in today's world is hard. People hurt our feelings, good and bad happens to everyone, and sometimes it can seem too much to bear alone. God built the family unit to be the foundation on which He grows and develops His church. As families, we have to work together to strengthen the other parts of the body. Talking together and praying together is the best way to accomplish this.

You will notice as a mommy that you will spend an amazing amount of time in the car. Sometimes you can feel like your main purpose in life is to shuttle kids from one activity to the next. Luckily, Mom's taxi can be designed to be a place where the kids know they are free to talk and share freely about their days. We can create this type of atmosphere by turning down the radio, and turning our cell phones off while we create conversations within the car. You may need to start by asking certain questions that will get them talking about what they are pondering in their hearts. Questions like *"What happened today that was awesome?"*, *"How was your math test today?"*, *"How did coach say you played?"*

U

Use Everything!

USE EVERY OPPORTUNITY TO TEACH

Titus 2:11-15
For the grace of God that brings salvation has appeared to all men. It teaches us to say "No" to ungodliness and worldly passions, and to live self-controlled upright and godly lives in this present age, while we wait for the blessed hope – the glorious appearing of our great God and Savior, Jesus Christ, who gave himself for us to redeem us from all wickedness and to purify for himself a people that are his very own, eager to do what is good.
These then, are the things you should teach."

As parents, we are called to be teachers. Teachers to our children and those individuals God places around us. We are called to be His mouthpiece to others, and speak the Word of God as if He were reading it off the pages in a sermon to us.

What if we aren't teachers? I truly believe that God gives many people the gift of intelligence in an area, but they might not know how to bestow that knowledge onto others. If they can't figure out relevant ways to share their wisdom with those around them, how can they do what it says in Titus and teach these lessons to those they have influence over?

I believe that the best lessons are learned by watching others. I learned how to take care of my children, not by my mom writing me a 10 step program, but by watching her raise us. I took bits and pieces from mothers that had a positive influence in my life, and I decided to sort of form my own way of mothering by emulating parts of all of them.

Once you create a sharing environment, your kids will just start talking about their days without needing much probing. Then you can show yourself to them as their biggest fan by actively listening, and giving advice when necessary. Take the time to talk. You will be amazed at what great things they have to say!

I have studied the Bible seriously for fourteen years, and have taken the Commandments and warnings from God's Word very seriously in my child rearing. I have repented for mistakes I have made as a mother, and each day I go to God asking Him to make me a better wife and mother. As mothers, our best way to teach our children how to say no to ungodliness, to live self-controlled, upright and godly lives in this present age is to live this way in front of them. The best way to teach our children to love God with all of their heart is to love God with our heart in front of them.

It's pure and simple. Less words, more action.

V

Vacation

ENJOY VACATIONS TOGETHER AS A FAMILY!

Psalm 37:3
Dwell in the land, and enjoy safe pasture.

One of the biggest mistakes we can make in life is never enjoying today, always preparing and planning for tomorrow. The only sure-fire thing in life we can plan on is the unexpected. We can save and put money away for retirement our entire lives, but what if we don't live until retirement age?

I am in no way, shape or form telling you to neglect planning for the future, but if in your planning you neglect living in the present, something is out of balance. There is an old saying that goes, *"No man on his deathbed would say he wished he'd spent more time at the office".* We all realize at one point in our lives what is really important: People! God has placed special people around all of us to love, encourage, spend time with and make memories with. As a parent, you are blessed with some of these little people living right in your home.

Vacations are awesome times to make memories together, take pictures that will tell stories for years, and recharge your souls in the Word so that you can continue living mission focused as a family. We need to be finding joy in our normal life, but the difference in vacationing is that they give us a free ticket to rest, play, avoid chores, eat a little more than normal, and have as little or as much schedule as you desire in doing so.

My family plans at least one vacation a year. We do not take expensive trips or live glamorously while we get away. We simply get away, and we do it together. We have taken the vow to never get too serious about ourselves or about life, and to know when God is calling us to rest and relax. Whether it is camping or flying oversees, it is simply important to unplug from the anxieties of life at least one or two weeks a year.

Life is uncertain.....eat a piece of cake!

Welcome Others

WELCOME OTHERS INTO YOUR HOME!

Romans 12:13
Share with God's people who are in need.
Practice Hospitality.

I love opening my home to others and making them feel welcome. Entertaining has always been something that my husband and I have done and loved to do. We love hosting birthday parties, picnics, Bible studies and dinners. Most of our best memories together as a family have been here at our home.

Gatherings at your house can become a stressful thing if you have the wrong outlook on hosting others. If we get hung up on perfection or people-pleasing, the joy can be snatched out from under us as quickly as we begin planning.

I used to work harder and longer cleaning and perfecting the house for gatherings than the gathering would even last. I am grateful God showed me how to include every family member in the preparation for the celebration, and in the clean up after. In doing this, our family all takes ownership of this blessing God gave us of a home.

It is important to my husband and me that we remember that everything that God has blessed us with belongs to Him and these things are only ours on loan. This helps us to keep things in perspective when KoolAid is spilled on the carpet, or nail polish on my daughter's white bedspread. We have to remind ourselves sometimes that people are more important than things.

We have tried to design our home to exude fun and relaxation. We desire that our kids and their friends want to be here so we can have the option of sharing Jesus with them. You may need to open your home, so others can open their hearts.

X

A few X words for encouragement!

EXamine your heart and **EXtinguish** sin so you can pursue **EXcellence**.

Don't **EXcasperate** yourself on the journey.

EXcactness in anything will never be achieved, but if the effort is **EXemplified**, the redeemer is glorified.

You are **EXactly** the woman He designed you to be.

EXude grace and dignity, and go that **EXtra** mile.

Exhilaration will occur when you begin to bear fruit.

EXcitement for the things of God will follow you on your walk.

EXplain to everyone the hope that you have, and **EXpect** great things for them.

Becoming an **EXpert** at living according to His Word, requires much **EXperience** on your knees.

Watch your **EXcuses**, and be careful who you **EXalt**!

I **EXhort** you to Love Jesus and set the **EXample** for others to follow.

Then when you make your **EXodus** from earth, there will be **EXhaltation** at your arrival in glory!

Y

YOU

YOU ARE IMPORTANT!

2Corinthians 6:16
...For we are the temple of the living God.
As God has said, "I will live with them
and walk among them,
and I will be their God and they will be my people."

One of the biggest mistakes we can make as Christian women, wives and mothers is to forget who we are. We have so many expectations placed on us to help and nurture others that we cannot sacrifice our own well-being when pursuing these goals.

Before I had children, I never understood why they tell you on airplanes to put the oxygen mask on yourself first then assist small children should there be an emergency. I used to think that sounded so selfish and backwards until I had been parenting for a few years. Nothing can make you less efficient as a wife and mother than burn-out. We are no good to our family when we are sick, tired and overworked. We cannot teach our children healthy habits if we are not practicing them ourselves. We cannot work effectively if we have not guarded with all diligence our minds and the bodies that God has given us. Our bodies are the temple of the Holy Spirit. In order to guard our witness for Christ and be able to run this marathon of life with excellence, we need to take care of ourselves.

Take an inventory of your daily habits. Are you eating properly, or drinking enough water? Do you exercise on a regular basis, and take vitamins? When was the last time you got a restful night's sleep or even an occasional nap? Do you get outside enough to enjoy some healthy sunshine that provides the Vitamin D that our bodies so desperately need?

When we are treating our bodies with the kind of care that God would desire us to, we are able to tackle the tasks He has for us. It is not selfish to care for yourself. You are the apple of God's eye. Have you had your apple today?

Z

Zoom In!

ZOOM IN ON PEOPLE!

Ephesians: 3:17-20
*"... And I pray that you, being rooted and established
in love, may have power, together with all the saints
to grasp how wide and long and high and deep
is the love of Christ, and to know this love
that surpasses knowledge - that you may be filled
to the measure of all the fullness of God."*

It is my prayer that you zoom in on the people in your snapshots of life. If there is anything I have learned from my husband over these past 20 years of marriage, it is how to take a good picture. I used to care more about the landmarks in the background that I was taking pictures of than the faces of the people that I visited these great places with. It seemed as if I just cared about crossing off places on my to-do list of life that I thought I needed to see before I die. I had been placing higher priorities on experiences than on my teammates in the experience. I don't live like that anymore and I pray that you never do. I pray that no matter what else you discover while you are here on earth, you discover the ultimate joy and satisfaction of loving God and loving people.

I pray you never take a single day for granted. I pray you forget about the tasks some days just to stop and play. I pray you eat a little bit of cake sometimes, and you laugh and dance like no one is watching.

I pray you find joy in serving the Lord and caring for your family. I pray your home is a safe and welcoming place that people desire to be. I pray you make more memories than you could have ever dreamed you would with those closest with you. I pray that you find beauty in the magnificent creature God calls you. Remember, He is crazy about you.

I pray you move in really close, decide not to care about the scenery in the back, and focus your heart lens on people. After all, this world's beauty has nothing on Heaven. You'll have an eternity there to sightsee.

I'll be busy though, staring at Jesus. God bless you.

MO MYDLO

Mo Mydlo has been happily married to Tommy Mydlo for twenty years. They reside in the Central Florida area with their four children and dog Tyco. Mo was ordained into ministry and served for six years as the Outreach Director for one of the fastest-growing Christian churches in the nation. Her new calling is to teach women how to renew their minds in the Word of God. She is releasing several books that will be available this year through Amazon. Mo is available to speak at women's groups, events and retreats. For more information about her schedule, please contact her at momydlo.wordpress.com. You can also follow Mo on Facebook and Twitter.

Made in the USA
Middletown, DE
17 March 2022

62771803R00035